# Sidereal Messenger

## A Book of Poetry

**Nicholas Wolf**

# Sidereal Messenger

## A book of Poetry

Nicholas Wolf

For information, contact:

info@wolfmont.com

or

**Wolfmont**
**238 Park Drive NE**
**Ranger, GA   30734**

**For Jeremy Charles Jackson**

And then shall he send his angels,
and shall gather together his elect
from the four winds, from the
uttermost part of the earth to the
uttermost part of heaven.

Mark 13:27

# PREFACE

All contemporary poets are faced with a dilemma; few readers will ever open a book of poetry, let alone read the great poets. So why write and publish books of poetry? For most of us, the readership is not a subject we think much about, though our wives get a good dose of our early efforts, and some friends are willing to receive an occasional shout.

Without a doubt, something is going on here that my friend, the amateur pianist, really doesn't put into words that make much sense; he plays almost everyday, just as he rows to the lighthouse every day. Wisdom says you can't make love every day, so maybe poetry or playing the piano, or rowing to the lighthouse is a likely substitute.

We write poetry because of the pleasure of making something out of nothing, and marvel at the result (or simply have to start over). We don't write every day; we scurry to find a scrap of paper when an idea or word or phrase comes into focus; it's like receiving the baton in a footrace.

Unfortunately we are pack rats with files and more files that say Poetry and are filled with scraps that didn't make the cut (beware the death of a poet and the bonfire that follows). The small amount of maple syrup that results from boiling down is exactly the same as the poem that started out with epic intentions and ends up a grain of wisdom or a moment of joy. That is why we write poetry!

Nicholas Wolf

# INTRODUCTION

What you have composed comes through as deceptively direct, down-to-earth, real, and resonant with some strong feelings of attachment and a healthy kind of nostalgia.

Is it poetry? What the hell IS poetry? My schoolboy indoctrination insisted on finding rhythm, rhyme, alliteration, metaphor, and a few other traits that could be pounced on in class and discussed *ad nauseum*. In college I was exposed to T.S. Elliot, free verse, and various "modern" approaches, all given the label of "poetic" by contemporary experts. The few "New Yorker" poems I try to stomach are all over the place with regard to form and meaning. All the old rules of grammar and diction seem to have to be flung overboard for anything to be classified as poetry these days.

So I would suggest that it is really irrelevant to determine whether or not you have written poetry. Be satisfied with creating some print that will have an effect on readers—it could be positive, interesting, provoking, maddening, or any number of other worthwhile reactions. Isn't that enough?


H. Kent Allen

# Table of Contents

Dedication ..................................................................i

Preface...................................................................iii

Introduction ..............................................................v

Sidereal Messenger .....................................................1

Absolute Abandon .......................................................2

Devout In Marigolds .....................................................3

I Miss Dialing My Son....................................................4

I Am Risen Indeed........................................................5

Clearing Out the Canopy................................................6

At the Meadow Stile: the Ram Captain.......................8

Atheism.....................................................................9

Adverse Possession....................................................10

A Pencil.....................................................................13

Tangible Personal Property .........................................14

Bums and Beggars......................................................15

Common Interest Agreement.........................................16

Blueberry Muffins .......................................................17

Impatient of Ghosts ....................................................18

In Thrall....................................................................21

Nothing of Consequence.............................................23

Leavings...................................................................24

Loss ........................................................................25

Rembrandt (dessinateur)..............................................27

Partsong...................................................................28

Photos......................................................................29

Rednecks ..................................................................30

Sometime After Cutting ...............................................31

The Create Zone ........................................................32

Tripolarity .................................................................33

Who .........................................................................35

Until the Penny Drops .................................................36

Upward.....................................................................37

Odd Endings .............................................................39

# Sidereal Messenger

And yet, it moves, he whispered,
While Earth settled the argument
In favor of God's favorite Church.
For who could deny, all standing:
Nothing moved, all stood firmly
Anchored, the Cardinal as well.

Then evening came; it was still.
The sun set, polite as could be.
To their credit, they condemned.
But saved by his own correction,
His formal abjuration, kneeling,
"Utter blasphemy," he stated.

He was sent under house arrest;
To his villa he must go,
A broken man, Galileo.

# Absolute Abandon

He walked away with the clothes on his back,
Started the car and drove 10 miles and parked
In a church lot, at the back of the church lot.
It was a Wednesday and no one was around.

He called his wife, said he had arrived at work,
Went into the woods and pulled out a gun,
Placed it in his mouth and pulled the trigger;
Last place they went looking was in the woods.

Three kids and a beautiful wife who loved him.
He loved her and the three kids, so the priest,
A family friend, had little to say that was helpful
To friends and family who crowded the pews.

These things happen: to you, to me: that is,
We park behind the church and sit there.
Maybe we get out of the car and walk into
The woods; maybe we cry, or curse, or
SHOUT!
Then we go home, hug the wife and kids
And go on with our lives.

# Devout in Marigolds

We planted Marigolds head to head,
Shouting they come from somewhere,
Everyone does, and it was perfect.

When they walked together after,
Hand in hand before what we knew,
On green lawns next to the Marigolds

I had no premonition - can it matter?
You and I will go on next and next
Devout in Marigolds no matter what.

# I Miss Dialing My Son

When can it ever happen without fear
That he may answer? I might call him,
Hold fast, and he answers, then what?
It's a bright day here, I'm figuring out
Where to go, what to do, take a jog.
His voice will always be the same:
Muscular with strong bones, and I?
Nothing is possible,
Thy hand alone.

# I Am Risen Indeed

They commandeer control central, trample
Your searing logic, delivered now in vain.
They are bright, smart, albeit courageous:
Scientists, fishermen, students, musicians.

Are they sealed from suffering and death?
Is there no violation when flesh is fleshly?
Their wind blows from thither to once upon.
But yet, God comes on heaven's breath.

Surely His testimony is from outermost
To this wise generation obscured by rote.
Dervishes also send siren calls by wire:
They are astray in fever and fantasy,

Has your wine lost its taste? Offer me bread
In obedience to your will; bind, stretch me
Until I touch the rim of your perfection.
Help me engage in those the devil holds.

If I meet your blessing and then turn away,
I am more than fool, not giving witness of You.
Make of me a Christ-like copy of your saints,
Then your promise is joy; I am risen indeed!

# Clearing Out the Canopy

Silence is part of these aerial acrobatics.
Listen, he shouts from below, look down at me
Or we're here all day, and he points his shears;
But looking down is precarious at thirty feet.

It's easy looking up when you climb a tree;
Looking down is terror - do I have a choice?
He points to my right: that's it, way out,
The skinny twig attached to the elbow.

Do you see the one, can you reach it?
I stretch out, stretch again ready for death.
You're practically there (easy for you to say,
Useless to argue). Please God, take me now!

I grab at the branch; it snaps off and drops.
Now don't look down; crawl toward the trunk.
Climbing the copper beech was fun, it was,
When I weighed nothing and lived forever.

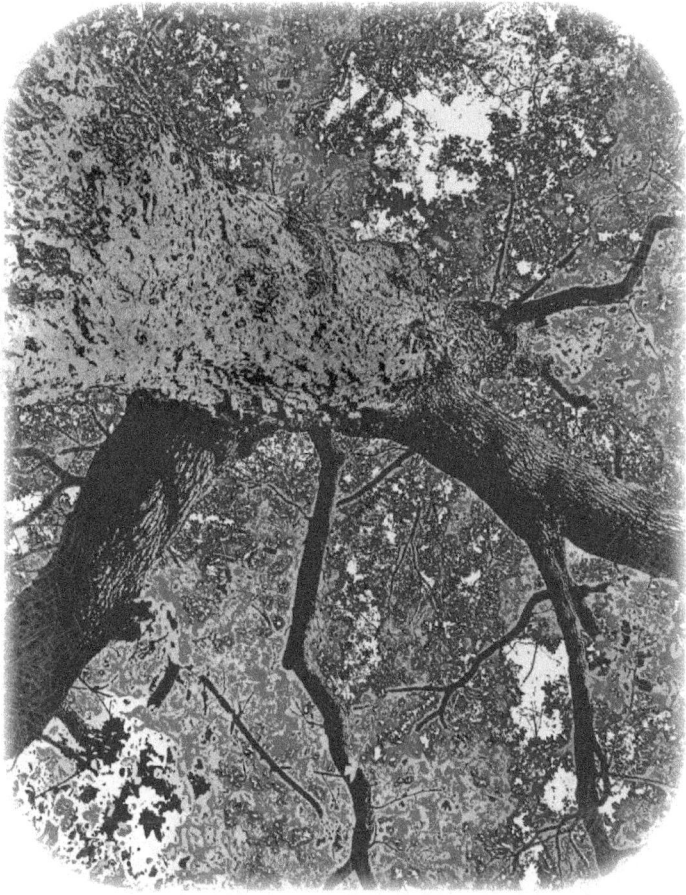

## At the Meadow Stile:
## the ram *Captain*

Two massive stones on edge along the fence are
Better than a gate to slip through should the ram
Decide a pail of grain is no warrant for intrusion.
Those were days: rain or shine, snow or sweat,
When the country boy became a man at dawn
And severed fear of Captain on a fenced in field.

New owners haven't pulled the backyard stones,
Or asked their neighbors for historical advice.
The fence is gone, the boy is gone, the ram
Was sold next door where farming lingered on:
Could the boy justify a trophy when he moved?
And so a faded photograph is all that's left

Of Captain, rest his soul.

# Atheism
## for CK

Getting in touch with his feelings
He robbed himself of several
Lifetimes that crossed his bow,
Worshiping human smallness
While styling his frail tinkering.

He was unaware his reality was
A closed system with imaginary
Windows and doors leading
Nowhere.

# Adverse Possession

My neighbor said he'd pay his share
But when a bill for fencing came
He said the color didn't satisfy,
And promptly built a fence the other
Side, one foot the other side of mine.
My lawyer said: remove your fence and
Occupy his land, unlikely he will know
Or care:

Measure well, yes, measure well!

# A Pencil

Give me a pencil and I will draw you a poem;
Read and pack the words in your knapsack.

They are arrows that will pierce you one day,
Songs of faith in you when I am down below,

A surfeit of precious cargo nestled within me,
But hurry, knot a pencil into our slipstream.

# Tangible Personal Property

At eighty-two on an autumn day he was urged
By his wife to deal with the cellar, nine boxes
Gathering dust, two waterlogged, an eyesore
Which upon his death would surely vanish
Into the yellow truck that swallowed treasure.

He had been reluctant to deal with the past,
But, an end in sight, he asked the handyman
To bring boxes up to a dark and vacant garage
Where they sat for three months of Sundays
Until his wife threatened to eliminate the lot.

In the fourth month he died, which was
What she feared would happen, though
Tuesdays, for nine long weeks, a box
Sat next to a bag of garbage curbside:
His ups and downs were lost forever.

# Bums and Beggars

Eager minds, soaring, in a fantasy of free love,
Plunged, rushed hungry into a restaurant and
Scraped food remains from plates, like shadows
Slipped out, sat down sprawled, and began to eat.

No guest showed interest but none had missed this
Invasion of sorts; they worried that once outside
The invasion would be personal or worse, say
A rude piss-off wisecrack, or a pitiful cry for coins.

Back at the office the incident was forgotten,
Though it turned up once at 3am, at home,
And turned up again as a brooding suspicion
That all was not right with this crazy world.

They held it at bay; one man ran for office.
A handbag was armed with ham sandwiches
To keep the boys and their girls from drugs.
We hoped they would come to their senses.

# Common Interest Agreement

They were married; well, not really married.
It's confusing; still, it was connubial bliss,
Skin in the game, including three children.

Logic says they had this common interest,
For, why do lovers sigh, and enjoy life?

But then, you know the rest of the story:
They told their friends, who quickly vanished.

Looking back, they had not been religious
So their common interest showed incredible
Maturity, sensitivity, and a quick separation.

# Blueberry Muffins
## for EB

She was, once upon a time
The young girl you see on
A swing in a far country.
At sixteen she took to sea,
And at nineteen
She was second mother to
Three small children who
Welcomed a firm friend.
The children lost her to a
Sailmaker with strong hands.

Each year just before
The Ides of March, that is,
Every year on his birthday
A card arrived first class,
Sometimes the only card:
She never forgot.

And so, on that rare occasion
When we have lost a friend
We are privileged to remember:
That love she gave us all;
Blueberry muffins and more.
Thanks be to God.

# Impatient of Ghosts

I am impatient of ghosts by day when you are here,
But when you go, I double lock the bedroom door
And try to cover up those signs of utter mayhem:
Strange pageants of sound, wild colors, dreams of
Certain death by poltergeist or slithering serpent.

When morning comes, and midday you return,
I am as brave and sure as you would have me be;
I say: "How was your trip, I slept right through -
I cut the grass and filed away, still missing you."
When night returns and you are here with me,

I am impatient of ghosts, and they are not here.

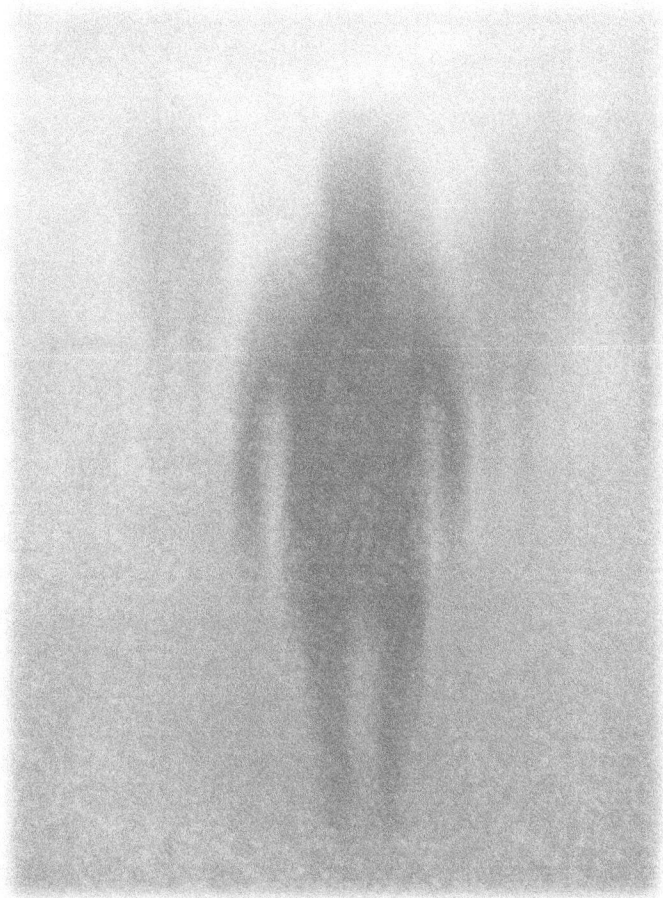

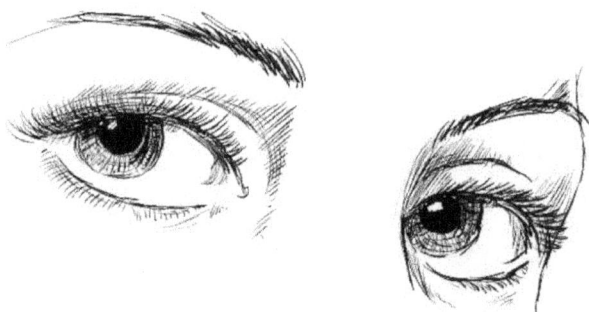

# In Thrall
## for PCMW

What remains under the shadow of her hat
Is a conspiracy of colors that skillfully
Cancel time - and her eyes, her eyes.

According to the time of day and
In spite of years (her youth long gone),
Catching inadvertently her smile,
Never lost to regrets:

What more could she say to me.

# Nothing of Consequence

There are no charred ruins here,
Just an empty house full of books,
Lavishly furnished in the old style
With a thermostat at fifty degrees.

The house is in the North; she winters in Florida.
Floor to ceiling volumes embrace what had been
His obsession, her husband the professor who
Died abroad at a conference before his time,
Unprepared as they both were for death.

I stay a week each winter and read his books
Coated in dust: I took a book two years ago
Then put it back last year before I left, though
Counting books would have come to nothing
As she reads the latest modern romances.

She was his assistant at the college; they married
And traveled to places he described at lectures;
They tried but had no children; he wrote books
And collected all sorts of leather-bound volumes.
She learned to cook and sew; she admired him.

# Leavings

Trash bags left roadside are
Filled with rotting memories
From the other side of time.

I am driving too fast on an icy road
In the chilled darkness heading south.
Two's company, but she likes the cold
And the grandkids - just as well.

There are times
And this is one of them.

# Loss

My soul is not soaring today;
I lost a friend this morning,
Not a relative, a close friend.
He had plans, excitement,

And dropped over dead.
How do you figure?
Do I move on, or cry
Over spilt friend?

The doctor said today
I had the knees of
A thirty year old,
So maybe there's time

To find a new friend,
Not an acquaintance.
But still, not soaring,
I lost a friend today.

## Rembrandt (dessinateur)

The lion stares at me; I am caught by
Dark eyes, his unruly headscarf that
Interrupts an intimate moment, when
Abruptly, you appear in the kitchen,
Where, not an early person, you say
Good morning, how did you sleep?

I am seized by heaving guilt, though
Brewing coffee is not particular to a
Season of guilt, or having thoughts
That bar entry are a category of sin.
The lion is no subject between us,
Or wasn't, except I have no answer.

# Partsong

We are a small ensemble, two alone.
I sing with you a repertoire that grows
By day and night; I watch your eyes,
Your lips, and hear your lovely voice.
Of love you say you will not sing,
But yes, our notes forever sing.

# Photos

Is there danger in sunny photos on dark days?
Better to see an elephant the blind man saw
Than confront oneself in the dawn of one's time
With angel locks, a body of marble and flint,
Owner of sand and sky, not a trace of bitter.

# Rednecks

Blood red is sixty percent of the land,
Blue is all the cities, forty percent, yet
In the boot room, what is paved takes.

The seagulls follow a blue trawler
Because they are hungry for sardines.
We are toothless hillbillies, fluff balls.

Don't matter who is your sugar Daddy:
On the Redneck Riviera with a view
We are All State and All American.

# Sometime After Cutting

Sometime after cutting, my quarter acre is filled
With simple flames of color; weeds are gone
And I am lashed with fantasy: a blazing bushfire
Of garish reds green and blue, an ancient brook,
An Eden, sweet colossus against the bitter end,
Unleashed in splendor, sometime before dying.

# The Create Zone

God's shadow? Not quite sure.
Disintermediation? Clever, maybe.
Rather, silent amid this hubbub,
Watch a tree get through the day
Or play checkers with a friend.
Life support is what it's all about
If you must know. But then again,
Choose your own poison or bliss.
Be original in the create zone.

# Tripolarity

Great ideas cover categories
Not yet invented or imagined.

Yet for now take a problem I
Have with your bizarre ideas:

My years of settled truth against
Your heaven on planet earth.

Could we meet above the clouds?

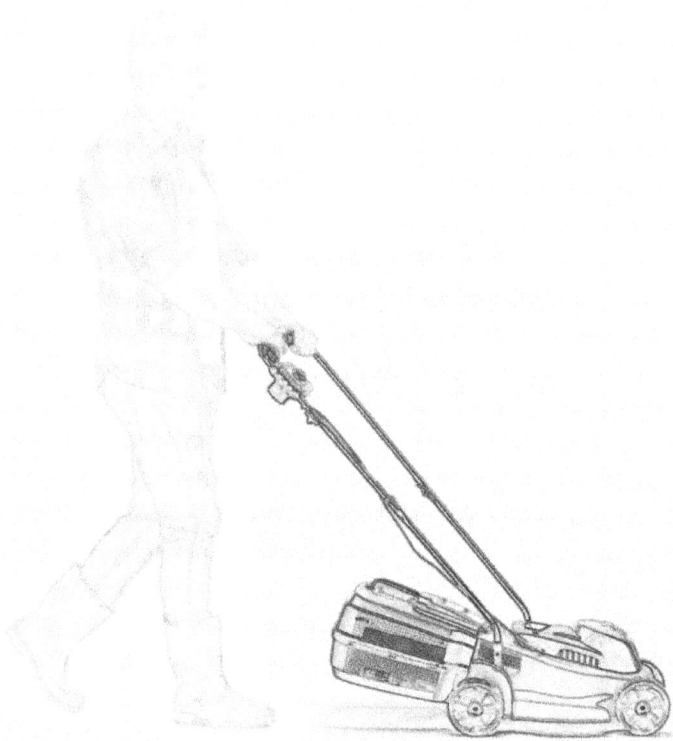

# Who

Who will wind the clocks when I am gone?
Who will care for her and mow the lawn
When I am gone?
Who will care for me and mend my socks
When she is gone?

# Until the Penny Drops

Get what scraps I can:
Green bean casserole,
Ultramarine waterfalls,
Meadow under the hill.

I am down, out of date;
Yet, in the realm of God,
Do what Thou would do:
Alight on my shoulder,

And speak so clearly
That even I will hear
What shall be likely:
The taste of your Son.

# Upward

Having done nothing extraordinary,
You will not be remembered;
Having done more than enough
You will be praised for
A vague notion of progress,
And forgotten.

I have your faded likeness
And think of you often.
Has a purer light marked the road?
Is your ceaseless walk close with Him?

# Odd Endings

The best ones die, yes they do,
In war or sickness or forgiven,
While I am here wondering
Does God really need them?

# * Notes *

# * Notes *